NOW THAT YOU ARE A CATHOLIC

To
my fellow Paulists
and to
the people and clergy
of Grand Rapids

Now That You
Are a Catholic
(Revised)

by

John J. Kenny
of the Paulist Fathers

PAULIST PRESS
New York / Paramus / Toronto

NIHIL OBSTAT:
Msgr. Joseph E. Shaw, S.T.L.
Censor Librorum

IMPRIMATUR:
✝ Joseph M. Breitenbeck
Bishop of Grand Rapids

May 16, 1973

The Nihil Obstat and Imprimatur are official declarations that a book or pamphlet is free of doctrinal or moral error. No implication is contained therein that those who have granted the Nihil Obstat and Imprimatur agree with the contents, opinions or statements expressed.

Library of Congress
Catalog Card Number: 73-80417

ISBN 0-8091-1743-6

Published by Paulist Press
Editorial Office: 1865 Broadway, N.Y., N.Y. 10023
Business Office: 400 Sette Drive, Paramus, N.J. 07652

Printed and bound in the
United States of America

Contents

I've just been baptized, but I don't seem to feel much different.

Introduction

You've just been baptized or made your profession of Catholic faith. Congratulations. You may have had to face opposition from old friends and relatives. Perhaps even some Catholics did not quite understand: "Why would anyone become a Catholic when the Church is in such a mess?"

But you focused on the important things. You know that the Church in its long history has gone through alternating periods of rest and unrest. It's a human institution and we expect that of anything human. But God saved us through the human nature of his Son and he continues his saving work through a human community of believers, the Church. He has called you to be a part of his community. We are human, you and I, and we are the Church.

This little book is not designed to give you more insight into the beliefs and history of the Catholic Church. You have a lifetime to explore the wonderland of belief and to examine the commoner ground on which the people of God has been wayfaring for centuries.

This book *is* designed to help you find your place in the community of believers as easily and conveniently as possible. You are already aware that the Church is a human family. It has customs, traditions and practices such as any large family or community has. Much of all this is related to Catholic belief, but much of it is just this family's way of doing things.

Lifetime Catholics have picked it up from parents, parochial school, Catholic friends and neighbors over a period of years, and it has become part of them. This is the easy way to learn. But this also makes it hard for a lifetime Catholic to separate what is essential from what is not. He may be shaken when an old tradition dies or when a familiar practice changes abruptly.

This book is a practical guide to the way things are done in the American Church. These are not necessarily the best ways; they do not come from some eternal decree of God. But you will want to know them and thus be able to thread your way through the maze. You will then be free to work at the serious (and, hopefully, joyous) business of being a Christian in this world and be able to profit most from what your religion has to offer.

The first part of the book is a series of "how to . . ." sections: "Going to Mass," "Getting Married," etc. The second section explains terms used in the American Church. Many of these terms refer to older practices familiar to lifetime Catholics. Some of the practices may never affect your life, but you will want to know what they are. There are also some newer terms which reflect the changes of the past ten years. The third section includes some of the common prayers and the Ten Commandments.

May you find all this helpful as you learn to know and love the Church, that community of which Jesus spoke when he said: "By this love you have for one another, everyone will know that you are my disciples."

Part I

1. Joining a Parish

Suddenly you are a member of the Catholic parish which includes your residence within its boundaries. "Who, me?" is an appropriate question. After all, you probably have no sense of formal affiliation with any parish yet. Maybe you intended to search out a particularly congenial place of worship. Has some local pastor drafted you? Fear not. Baptism, Church law and geography have just combined to put you in one parish instead of another one. Like most Catholics, you may find yourself thoroughly at home in the parish which embraces you geographically. If not, you can worship in another parish. It's as simple as that.

Then why bring up membership in the local territorial parish? There are practical and informational reasons for that. The practical reason is that certain functions usually are reserved by the parish in which you live: for example, baptisms, marriages and funerals. If Church law were interpreted inflexibly, that might be that. However, in most places the spirit of the law is the important thing, and exceptions are made when necessary.

The informational reasons have to do with history and social developments. It is worthwhile knowing that the Roman Catholic Church is composed of many large territorial sections called dioceses, each presided over by a bishop. Every diocese has territorial subdivisions called parishes, each presided over by a priest called a pastor. All this is very tidy. It is the exceptions which complicate things.

Take "national" parishes. In the United States many parishes were originally established to serve ethnic groups rather than everybody within specified territorial boundaries. This was necessary to take care of the large numbers of immigrants who came from Europe during the nineteenth and early twentieth centuries. Though the Mass was said in Latin, sermons, announcements and parish business were done in Polish, Italian, Slovak or German.

Many of the "national" parishes have become territorial parishes or have closed down. But you may still find a Lithuanian or French national parish (or, currently, a Spanish parish) where some or all of the Masses are celebrated in the language of the ethnic group. A member of that ethnic group may substitute the national parish for his territorial parish, and he has full access to the adopted parish for the purposes usually reserved by the territorial parish (i.e., baptism, marriage, funerals, etc.).

The university parish is a recent development. If you are a student or teacher at certain universities, you can become a member of the parish established specifically for the university community. Of course, a student or teacher may choose to remain a member of his territorial parish.

Many university religious centers are not parishes, though they perform certain parish functions. Near large urban centers you may also find "floating" or "underground" worshiping groups. Some of these are approved by the local bishop and some are not.

A further complication: a million Catholics in the

United States belong to the Eastern rites of the Church. The people who belong to Eastern rite parishes have bishops of their own whose dioceses may cover a very large section of the United States. The ancestors of these people came from Eastern Europe, especially the Ukraine, and from the Near East, especially Lebanon. Words like Byzantine Rite, Ruthenian, Greek Catholic, Maronite or Melkite identify these groups.

You are welcome to attend Mass and receive Communion in these churches. But, thanks to a quirk of history, you are not supposed to join one of these parishes unless you were received into the Catholic Church by a priest of an Eastern rite. Such churches are easily confused with the independent Eastern Churches such as the Greek Orthodox Church or the Armenian Church.

At this point, you may feel the need for a rule of thumb. This one has the advantage of simplicity: unless you are associated with a university or have a strong ethnic attachment, the logical move is to try the local territorial parish first. The great majority of American Catholics go to Mass, receive the sacraments and participate in religious activities of the parish in which they live.

By asking a Catholic neighbor or by calling up the parish office, you can find out what times Mass is celebrated. At Mass you will receive a bulletin which lists the names of the priests, times of Mass, times of other religious services and the parish activities for the week.

You may want to register officially in the parish. Most parishes have a register of parishioners and an envelope system for church contributions. The envelope system is a convenience for the parish, but it also will help you at income tax time.

As far as financial support is concerned, be generous. Figure out what a fair share would be and give a bit more if you can. Some parishes have a large debt or may be operating a parochial school. The health of a parish community depends to a great extent on the generosity of its responsible parishioners.

Registering in the parish will give you an opportunity to meet your parish priests. You can telephone the rectory and make an appointment. Priests enjoy meeting a new parishioner, particularly a convert. And the priest may prove to be a real help in your adjustment to parish life.

But what if plunging in seems too much all at once? Then feel no immediate obligation to immerse yourself in parish activities. Furthermore, if you should find that you are not at home in the local parish, for some reason, you owe no one an explanation. As a Catholic, you are free to attend Mass wherever you want. The essential thing is for you to find a community where you can join joyously in liturgical celebration. If you have to go outside your territorial parish to achieve this, go where your spirit is best nourished.

Then any parish involvement will grow out of the sense of Christian brotherhood nurtured by this shared eucharistic experience.

2. Going to Mass

The Last Supper was a simple gathering. Its significant words and gestures could be done in a few minutes. We are not surprised to learn that over the centuries, the Church has developed this simple rite into a much more elaborate ceremony. But the Mass remains what it always was. The Church does what Jesus did at the Last Supper; she celebrates the first coming, the life, death, resurrection and second coming of God's only Son.

This chapter is written, not to help you gain more insight into the significance of the Mass, but to help you with the many details involved in the way it is celebrated today.

As a beginning, it is good to plan to arrive early for Mass, but not so early that you find the parking lot filled with cars from an earlier Mass. Getting to church about ten minutes before Mass is just about right.

Upon entering the church, most Catholics dip the fingertips of their right hand into the holy water font and make the sign of the cross. This is a traditional reminder of baptism and the Christian's new life in Christ.

After blessing yourself, you may be shocked to find a man sitting at a table who asks you for twenty-five cents "seat money." This is rare today; it is a relic of the times when most parishes were financed this way.

My wife was surely happy to learn that the Greeting of Peace is a handshake, not a kiss.

Where do you sit? In Catholic churches it is rare to find any pews reserved. You can choose anyone you like. The front quarter of the church offers the best opportunity for full participation in the Mass. If you are concerned about when to stand, sit or kneel, you can avoid the front row or two and count on watching the movements of somebody up front who looks confidently Catholic. If you are worried about disturbances from your children, you can see if the church has a "cry room." Of course, normal restlessness on the part of children should be expected by priest and people. A cry room is primarily for those whose children are too young to avoid memorable disturbances.

In most churches it is customary to genuflect before entering a pew. You touch your right knee to the floor as kind of a bow to Jesus, present in the Eucharist. In some parishes, the tabernacle containing the Eucharist will not be on the main altar, and people may not genuflect. However, the traditional practice of going down on one knee is still the common practice.

You may see some people making the sign of the cross and striking their breast while genuflecting. This is not necessary.

On entering a pew, Catholics usually kneel in prayer a few moments before sitting down. This can help you prepare for worship. It can also be hard on the knees if you don't check the kneeler. It should be swung down to provide a proper surface for tender shinbones. Do not be surprised to see people who arrive late pausing to kneel down even though the rest of the congregation is standing or sitting.

You probably will find a "missalette" or Mass book awaiting you in the pew. Such booklets are of limited usefulness. Designed to permit the congregation to read every word of the Mass, they can divert people from spontaneous participation in the liturgy. What you need from the booklet are the words of hymns, the Gloria and the Creed. Hymns are no problem because they are announced by number and page. The Gloria and Creed are found in the first pages of text and do not require strenuous hunting down.

You can learn all the other prayers and responses by listening to them and perhaps repeating them quietly just a bit behind the rest of the congregation. Trying to do everything "by the book" is distracting. If the booklet fascinates you, it is no crime to borrow a paper-bound missalette. At home you can go over what was done at Mass if you find that helpful.

Unless you always attend Mass in the same church with the same priest, you can expect some variety in the way things are done. If a Mass is labeled "folk" or "contemporary" in the parish bulletin, you can expect it to be livelier than the customary Mass.

Usually an entrance hymn greets the priest and his assistants as they enter the church. The people stand to sing as the priest approaches the altar. Sometimes there is no music or hymn. And in some places, the priest has no assistants and is alone on the altar until Communion is distributed. You will soon discover what is customary in your parish.

There is no reason to feel conspicuous if you hesitate before following the standing, sitting and kneeling of the congregation. Only you will know that you are responding hesitantly. The naturally slow risers, sitters and kneelers will make your actions seem quite timely. The reasons for standing, sitting or kneeling will become apparent as you get familiar with the procedures of the Mass.

After a brief introductory rite, which includes an admission of sin, the Gloria and the prayer of the day, the Mass proceeds into its two main parts: the Liturgy of the Word of God and the Liturgy of the Eucharist.

The Liturgy of the Word of God comes first. In it, God's word comes to the congregation through readings from the Bible and in the priest's sermon. The people respond to God's word in ways that will slip naturally into your memory.

To elaborate a bit, at Sunday Masses there are three readings from the Bible. The first is from the Old Testament, the second from any part of the New Testament other than the Gospels, and the third from one of the four Gospels. A layman called a "lector" usually does the first two readings while the people remain seated. The congregation recites or sings the responses.

The people stand during the priest's reading of the Gospel. Standing serves as an expression of respect for the words and life of Jesus. Priest and people make a gesture at the beginning of the reading: a small sign of the cross is made with the thumb on the forehead, mouth and breast. It is a prayer that God will impress the words of the Gospel on our minds, on our lips and in our hearts. The sermon, called a "homily," follows. The people's response usually is the Nicene Creed, a fifth century formulation of Catholic belief. Next comes the "Prayer of the Faithful" or the "Bidding Prayers," prayers for the needs of the Church, the world and the local community. On some occasions, in some parishes, the people add their own spontaneous prayer petitions. The Prayer of the Faithful concludes the Liturgy of the Word of God.

The Liturgy of the Eucharist follows. The Eucharist is simply doing what Jesus did at the Last Supper.

Everything else is the current form of liturgical elaboration.

The offertory comes first. During this time, the bread (usually shaped into small discs called "hosts"), the cup or chalice, and cruets of wine and water are brought to the altar. A hymn is usually sung and the collection is taken up. The offertory includes the setting of the table for the Eucharist.

The eucharistic celebration begins with the "Preface," concluding with the "Holy, Holy, Holy" recited by all. The Canon comes next. It is the long eucharistic prayer spoken by the priest. During the Canon the priest recalls the words and acts of Jesus at the Last Supper.

At the key point of the Canon, the priest uses the actual words of Jesus: "This is my body . . ., this the cup of my blood." It is at this moment, called the "Consecration," that bread and wine become the body and blood of Christ. The priest holds up the consecrated host and the chalice and asks all to "proclaim the mystery of faith." The response of the people will soon be familiar to you.

The Canon continues with prayers for different groups of people and individuals. It concludes with the priest holding up the body and blood, together. The people recite or sing the "great Amen."

The Lord's Prayer with a long conclusion follows. Then comes the greeting of peace. The exchange of greetings of peace is new to American Catholics. You simply shake hands with those around you and say, "Peace be with you" or something like it. There are people who will ignore you, but their number is dwindling. In many parishes, greetings run forward, backward and to both sides, and the priest and his assistants may join in the handshaking and expressions of Christian warmth.

Communion itself is important enough to merit a separate chapter. It is enough here to indicate what follows Communion: a final prayer, the blessing (to which the people respond by blessing themselves), a word of dismissal and a final hymn. When the longer solemn blessing is used, it is appropriate to answer "Amen" to each of the three parts.

Some Catholics linger to say prayers of thanksgiving after Mass. Often, members of the congregation and the priest pause to talk to one another outside the church. But in every parish there are those who seem to be in a terrible hurry. You may wonder what the urgency is, but after all it does take all kinds to make a parish.

3. Receiving Communion

Catholics believe that Communion is an encounter with Christ himself. This belief is rooted in the New Testament and nurtured by centuries of consistent teaching. In a sense, there is no closer union possible with Christ on this earth than in that unique moment of Communion.

This is not to make Communion an individualist "just Jesus and me" sort of thing. Notice that the word used is "Communion" (rather than simply "union"). The sacrament, in uniting us to Jesus, unites us to each other.

Because Catholics take the matter of Communion so seriously, they often have strong feelings about the way it is administered. It is not unusual for some Catholics, older people usually, to say that it is "irreverent" for the host to be placed in the hand instead of on the tongue. On the other hand, you have the "host-grabber" who insists on Communion in the hand even in places where it is not the common practice.

This chapter is designed to familiarize you with the Church's rules on Communion and the ways it is administered. This will leave you free to concentrate on the important thing, the encounter with Jesus himself.

You may already have noticed one difference in terminology. In Protestant Churches, people speak of "taking" Communion. Catholics "receive" Communion. The difference is not important, but you can bear it in mind.

Normally a Catholic will want to receive Communion at every Mass he attends. You should not receive Communion twice the same day unless you have a good reason for doing so. Here's an example. You receive Communion at a wedding on Saturday morning out of affection for the bride and groom. You can certainly receive again at the regular parish Saturday evening Mass.

You may meet misinformed Catholics who claim that you must go to confession every time you go to Communion. Only in cases where you have sinned so seriously as to break your relationship to God are you expected to seek sacramental forgiveness before receiving Communion.

Years ago the Church had a strict law about fasting from midnight before Communion. The law has been gradually modified. Now the only requirement is that you eat or drink nothing but water for an hour before the time of Communion. This presents little difficulty, considering that it takes you some time to get to church, and it takes forty minutes or so of the Mass before Communion is distributed.

Now let us come to the Communion part of the Mass. The priest holds up the consecrated host, saying, "This is the Lamb of God. . . ." The people answer, "Lord, I am not worthy. . . ." The priest receives Communion first. If Communion is to be given out under the form of bread only, he drinks the contents of the chalice. If the congregation is large, another priest, a deacon, or a specially delegated layman or laywoman may help distribute Communion. The people usually sing a hymn during Communion. If you don't know the words, it is appropriate to bring the Mass booklet with you to the altar.

Before going up for Communion, you may want to watch some of the other communicants. You can then see how Communion is administered in this church and at this Mass. There are differences.

The first variation you may notice is whether the people kneel or stand for Communion. Pedantic Catholics argue over such things. Kneeling is more "reverent," or standing emphasizes the "dignity of the Christian." Happily, the debate is not likely to be carried on during Communion. If the issue comes up elsewhere, you may want to remind the debaters that at the Last Supper the Apostles received Communion lying on couches.

If Communion is received kneeling, the communicants kneel along the Communion rail or the edge of the sanctuary. The priest moves from person to person, then returns to the starting point and begins again. If you stay in the regular flow of traffic, there will be no problem. If Communion is received standing, the people form lines and wait their turn to approach the priest who remains in one place.

Now we come to the moment of Communion itself. The typical procedure is this: The priest holds up the host and says, "The Body of Christ." You answer, "Amen." You offer your tongue not quite as dramatically as you do when you are having your throat examined. The priest then places the host on your tongue. You close your mouth and move away. Pay no attention to people who tell you it's a sin to bite the host. The body of Christ is food and is meant to be eaten as such.

In some places the communicant is given the option of receiving the host on the tongue or in the hand. You will want to offer either your hand or your tongue obviously enough to let the priest know how you prefer to receive the host.

Intinction is another approach to distributing Communion. The method is not usually used with large Sunday congregations. Intinction is simple enough if everyone receives on the tongue. The priest holds up the host and says, "The Body and Blood of Christ." You answer, "Amen." The priest then dips the host into the chalice of wine and places the host on your tongue.

Intinction gets complicated when a minority want to receive Communion in the hand. The priest may have dipped the host before he sees the expectant hand. Either you get the soggy host in your hand, or you let him put it in your mouth. In a situation where all the people expect the host in the hand, intinction is accomplished readily. The priest holds up the host and says, "The Body and Blood of Christ." You answer, "Amen." He puts the host in your hand, and you dip it in the chalice. There is an answer to everything. And sometimes several.

In Masses for small groups the priest sometimes invites the people to drink from the chalice itself. The rim of the chalice is wiped off before it is passed from one communicant to another. It is hard to prescribe rules for small group Masses. In these situations, do what everybody else does.

No matter how Communion is administered—kneeling, standing, sitting at a table—whether it's the tiny white host or a chunk of Syrian bread with a healthy sip of Burgundy wine—it is Jesus you are meeting, it is Jesus who nourishes you and invites you closer to himself and to your fellow Christians. The heart of the matter is the encounter with Jesus. If you find that encounter the rarest of experiences, you are not alone.

My first confession
must have been very
harrowing for you, eh?

4. Receiving Sacramental Forgiveness

Most Catholics do not like to go to confession. Most priests do not enjoy hearing confessions. This general dissatisfaction with the sacrament is one of the reasons why in 1977 a new "Rite of Penance" replaced the older form. As a result, Catholics are beginning to speak more about the "sacrament of reconciliation" and less about "going to confession."

You as a new Catholic may have serious reservations about this sacrament, no matter what it's called. It may still seem like a visit to a dentist's chair. Yet surely a merciful God is ever ready to forgive, so why not go to him and save a lot of wear and tear on everybody?

There are some good reasons for the sacrament. Let's start with the experience of human reconciliation. Have you ever broken your friendship with anyone and wanted to restore it? How awkward it is to approach the other person! How should I go about it? What words should I use? How hard it is to admit I was wrong! How can I explain the excuses I used to justify the break? How afraid I am of being rejected! How embarrassing all this is to me and to the other person!

Yet these awkward feelings are the very stuff of human relations. I am real and the other person is real.

What a magnificent moment this is! The veneers and superficialities fall off and we reveal ourselves as weak and trembling human beings, seeking love and reconciliation.

The sacrament of reconciliation begins with this basic human experience. After all, our sin is not so much a matter of offending God as it is harming or hurting our fellow human beings. This human dimension of the sacrament is important.

Why a priest then? The priest in this case represents the Church. Our sin may harm certain specific people, but it also hurts the Church. As Christians we are members of a community of faith, in this case the Catholic Church. Our sin gives this community a bad name and harms it in other ways. Thus we need reconciliation with the Church.

Finally, God makes use of this sacrament of reconciliation to reconcile sinners to himself. Such has been the traditional teaching of the Church. "If you forgive the sins of any, they are forgiven" (John 20: 23). In this sacrament, then, there is forgiveness and reconciliation with God, with the Church and in some way with our fellow human beings.

This indicates why the Church considers the sacrament fundamental, but it does not make clear how often you should seek sacramental forgiveness. As a new Catholic you might want to celebrate the sacrament before Christmas and Easter and perhaps at other times of the year. How often will depend on two factors: (1) if you find yourself falling into patterns of serious sin; (2) how helpful you find the sacrament in keeping you oriented toward Christian values.

Catholics used to make a sharp distinction between "mortal" (serious) and "venial" (less serious) sin.

The distinction may still be helpful in some cases. However, many Catholics had developed a trivialized or taboo notion of sin. Often there was a list of sins to consult, with mortal and venial sins checked off before confession. Such an attitude is betrayed in statements like: "I think it's all right, but the Church says it's a sin." Sin has become something external to them, something that happens to them, not a freely chosen harmful way of acting.

Sin, especially serious sin, is a pattern of conduct (or, at times, a single action) that reflects a choice of some value other than God or the good of others. We may choose power, wealth, pleasure, ease, success or ego gratification and make it the dominant value of our life. If we have made this choice or are well on the way to doing so, the sacrament of reconciliation is the answer.

Even if you are not drifting into anything this fundamental, you might find confession helpful from time to time. It can aid you to re-examine your way of life, to measure your growth in the love of God and neighbor and to identify any habits of selfishness that may be hindering Christian development. Many Catholics find that the sacrament serves this purpose well.

In addition to the better-known private confession or "rite of individual reconciliation," there is a communal form of the sacrament. The communal celebration is a church service with hymns, prayers, readings from Scripture, a homily and other features. There is a point in the service where people are invited to confess individually. In rare cases where the crowd is too large for the number of priests available, a general confession and absolution conclude the service.

The communal form is part of an effort to restore a

community dimension to the sacrament. It gets away from the anonymity, the rigidity and the focusing of communal responsibility on one man, the priest, that were characteristic of the older form of private confession. When the opportunity to participate in a communal penance service is offered, you might want to try it.

Individual confession is still much more common than the communal form and merits some discussion. Though it is possible to make an appointment with a priest for confession, most people go at the regularly scheduled hours. You can consult the parish bulletin or call the rectory to find out when these are. It is perfectly acceptable to shop around for a priest who you think will be sympathetic and understanding. The priest who hears your confession is called, oddly enough, the confessor. You are the penitent.

Before confessing, it is helpful to go over in your mind what you want to say. This "examination of conscience" should be a realistic appraisal of your spiritual condition, focusing on sinful habits and on any serious sin committed since your last confession. A proper penitential spirit is evident when you're open and honest about your shortcomings and determined to change for the better.

When confessing, be matter-of-fact and succinct. If you have something serious to confess, you may want to give it emphasis by bringing it up first or last. If your sin is a habitual attitude, such as a consistent hatred for someone, indicate that it is more than a passing feeling. If your sins are specific actions, there is no need to give an absolutely accurate count. Your concern should be to distinguish isolated instances from repeated patterns.

Here are a few hints on confessing:

1. Confess your own sins, not somebody else's: "You see, Father, my husband drinks. . ."

2. There is no need to tell a long rambling story: "Father, I was in this bar and in comes this blonde who sits down next to me. . ."

3. Don't worry about shocking your confessor: "His ears will burn when he hears what I have to say." He's heard it all before.

The New Rite of Penance calls for a setting quite different from the old confessionals. A new "reconciliation room" has at least these two features: a kneeler and screen for those who prefer to be anonymous, and a chair located in such a way that the person can converse with the priest face to face. There may be a table with a Bible and some other furnishings. When you enter, you simply make the basic choice of kneeling behind the screen or sitting in the chair.

In this period of transition, many churches will not yet have a reconciliation room and will still be using the old confessionals. Each confessional usually has three enclosed sections in it. The priest sits in the middle enclosure; penitents kneel on either side. An electric light system may help you determine when the sections are occupied. At times a line will form on either side, and penitents are expected to wait their turn.

When a penitent's section is free, you go in and kneel down, closing the door or curtain after you. If the priest is busy with a penitent on the other side, the shutter on your side will be closed. When he finishes, he will open the shutter on your side. A screen or curtain separates you from him. This opening of the shutter is an obvious gesture, and you will know it is time to begin. If it isn't that obvious, the priest will say something to let you know he is ready.

The New Rite of Individual Reconciliation is outlined here for you. Though it may seem highly structured and formal, it is meant to be relaxed and conversational. After preparing yourself beforehand and waiting your turn, if need be, you enter the room or confessional and sit or kneel.

1. *Welcome*. The priest greets you and you respond. You make the sign of the cross, audibly.

2. *God's Word*. At your initiative or the priest's you or he may read a passage of Scripture and discuss it together. Passages dealing with the healing or forgiving power of Jesus are preferred. Many priests are not ready for this yet, and you may not be up to it. This part is optional.

3. *Confession*. It's customary to mention how long it has been since your last confession. Feel free to bring up any doubts or questions. The priest is there to help you, not scold you.

4. *The Penance*. In response to your confession, the priest may offer you a word of advice or encouragement. He will ask you to do a "penance" or satisfaction, a token prayer or action as an expression of your desire to make amends. If it's a prayer you've never heard of or an action that would be unusually difficult for you, explain this to the priest and he will change it to something else. The penance is not done at this point, but afterward.

5. *Act of Contrition*. At this point you express your sorrow for sin by a prayer. It can be a spontaneous one of your own, or one of the many recommended for the

New Rite. You can use the "Act of Contrition" from the back of this book.

6. *Absolution*. The priest will extend his hand over your head and recite the prayer expressing your forgiveness. It concludes with the sign of the cross. You respond: "Amen."

7. *Conclusion*. The priest prays: "Give thanks to the Lord for he is good." You respond: "His mercy endures forever." The priest gives a pleasant word of farewell and you reply in kind. You walk out knowing that you are really forgiven, that you've made a new start, and that, believe it or not, you can look God himself in the eye!

Your First Confession

There are two kinds of first confessions. The first type is that of someone who was baptized in another · Christian church. If this is your situation, you know that you make your first confession and profession of faith as part of your admission into the Catholic Church. Where conditional baptism is required (in case of serious doubt as to whether you were baptized before or not), the same confessional procedure is followed.

Some people panic when they learn that this first confession is to cover all sins committed since baptism. If you were baptized as a baby, it means confessing the sins of a lifetime. However, the confession need not be an exhaustive laundry list; only significant things should be mentioned. Confess only what you thought was sinful at the time. Knowledge and insight that came later are not retroactive.

The priest who instructed you will offer guidance.

He may hear your confession himself, or he may make an appointment with another priest for you. In any case, you simply follow the procedure outlined earlier. If the stages of the New Rite seem hopelessly confusing to you, just go in and tell the priest that this is your first confession and that you're in the process of being received into the Church. Let him take it from there. Fingernail biting is unnecessary. The priest is on your side, and he knows how difficult a first confession can be.

The second kind of first confession is that of someone who is received into the Catholic Church by baptism. There is no difficulty here. Since baptism is the primary sacrament for the forgiveness of sin, all sins of your past life are forgiven by this baptism. Sins committed before baptism are never confessed in the sacrament of penance. You may receive your First Communion immediately after baptism.

There is one bit of advice that can be helpful here. Don't wait a very long time before making your first confession. If you keep putting it off, the day may come when you really need it, and it will look like a big high wall to climb over. If you make your first confession when you have only a few small things to confess, you can be relaxed about it and enjoy the experience.

5. Getting Married

"Two become one body" was the way Jesus described marriage. "Two become frantic" is the way some couples remember their wedding preparations. Marriage is one of the great moments in your life, and you want everything to be just right.

In making your preparations for marriage, include the Church early in your plans. Don't pick a date, rent a hall or send out invitations before you consult the priest. Often a priest has many weddings on his schedule. He may not be able to give your wedding the time and attention it deserves unless you give him adequate notice. Six weeks is usually a safe margin, but visit the rectory earlier if you can.

If You Marry a Catholic

Catholic Church practice calls for the wedding to take place in the parish of the bride. A convert can readily get the practice reversed. While it should prove easy to have the wedding arranged in the parish of your intended, you should check out any alternate plans early. Some parishes are reluctant to give permission for a marriage to be celebrated in a parish other than the traditionally appropriate places.

There are guidelines for priests to follow in preparing a couple for a wedding, but practices vary from parish to parish. The priest will talk with you, ask questions frankly designed to discourage those who are unready for sacramental marriage, and try to find out if there are any foreseeable marital problems. There will be documents to obtain, forms to fill out. Some of this is just the bureaucratic officiousness of any large organization. Part is due to the Church's real concern that you are properly prepared to live a lifetime together. Concern is Christian and appropriate. A lifetime can be a long time.

Preferably the couple will come together for any sessions with the priest. If really necessary, especially if you and your intended live far apart, another priest can see one of you and do part of the preparatory work. This complicates things and consumes extra time. In many areas, "Pre-Cana conferences" are given for engaged couples. Such conferences are conducted by doctors, counselors and experienced couples who do a good job of putting marriage in the Christian context.

Both of you will be asked to produce a baptismal certificate authenticated within six months of the wedding. For a convert, a certificate of profession of faith with its notation of non-Catholic baptism is an equivalent. You can get the certificate from the place where you were received into the Church.

Both of you also may be asked to fill out a long questionnaire. The questions cover some commonplace facts, your understanding of what marriage means, any possible obstacles (impediments) in Church or civil law, and your willingness to marry free of undue pressure. Often the priest will talk separately with each partner, ask the questions and write down the responses. You read and sign the questionnaire at the end of the interview. The priest may ask you to take an oath on the Bible that what you have said is true. Some priests find the routine a bit oppressive and settle for their own feeling as to the truthfulness of the parties. But even some who find the oath inappropriate feel obliged to ask for it.

There is an additional procedure that is quite common. You may be asked to have one or two people who know you well (usually your parents) come in to see the priest and fill out another form. The purpose of the form is to get further testimony to the fact that you are free to marry (that is, that you have not already been married to somebody else). As a convert, you may be reluctant to ask somebody, especially a non-Catholic, to do this. It may help you to know that the procedure rarely takes more than five minutes of a witness' time.

The procedures described usually are all that is required. Occasionally there are special permissions called for or other matters that take extra time. Some couples want to have a priest friend from elsewhere come in to do the wedding. Usually this can be arranged easily, but it is wise to ask both the friend and the local priest early. If the priest is from out of state, you will want to find out if your state has any legal requirements that complicate this. You must also have your blood test and obtain the wedding license. State and Church combine to give you quite a workout. The "banns," an official announcement of your wedding, do not add to your burdens: without effort on your part, they are published on three successive Sundays in the parishes of both parties before the wedding.

With the red tape behind you, you can get down to what really interests you. The new Catholic marriage rite is a beautiful and flexible one. There are alternate forms of the prayers and blessings, and you have a wide choice of the Scripture readings. You can express your marriage vows without repeating them phrase by phrase after the priest, if you like. The priest will have a booklet to show you the variety of choices open to you. You can plan with him a ceremony which seems particularly suitable to you.

You may have a wedding with or without a Nuptial Mass. The Nuptial Mass is beautiful and offers you more choices of variables. Most Catholics want it. However, sometimes a convert's family would be uncomfortable with a Mass. Rather than have them feel less than perfectly at home, the convert may choose to have a simple wedding ceremony. Still, by talking over a sticky situation with the priest, you probably can get him to give a brief homily which explains the Mass and makes the non-Catholic family feel welcome.

Usually you can have the kind of music you want at your wedding, even guitars. Sometimes, though, there are diocesan and parish rules on this and other matters.

Most Catholic weddings are held on Saturdays. This may limit your choice of a wedding time somewhat: parish Saturday evening Mass and confessions have to be taken into account. There is a standard fee for a wedding, and it is appropriate for you to ask what it is and what it covers. Anything you may wish to give the priest is separate from the standard fee.

A rehearsal is usually held the evening before the wedding. This is a time when it is important to have the full wedding party get to church on time. Otherwise, more than the priest may be delayed. Other rehearsals may be scheduled for the same night. Church law does *not* require that the two official witnesses (the best man and the maid of honor) be Catholics. At the rehearsal the priest usually will make himself available for any in the wedding party who want to go to confession.

If You Marry a Non-Catholic

If you plan to marry someone who is not a Catholic, the procedure is pretty much the same. The wedding ordinarily would take place in your parish. Six hours of instruction for the couple are a common requirement. The content and format of the instruction varies from place to place.

The Catholic party must promise to do his best to raise the children as Catholics. The non-Catholic party is no longer asked to do so; he is simply informed that his partner has done this. A couple should discuss this matter thoroughly and reach some agreement before it comes up at the priest's house.

You may prefer a wedding without a Mass when both families are mostly non-Catholic. But if a Mass would be acceptable, why miss it? A non-Catholic, even the bride or groom, is not allowed to receive Communion without special permission of the bishop. Such permission is rarely given. Church law does allow a clergyman of another faith to take some part in the service. This can be a bit delicate, depending on the priest and the other clergyman you have in mind.

Two wedding ceremonies, one in the Catholic Church and the other elsewhere, are not allowed. But a Catholic can be married in a ceremony in another church or synagogue or even before a civil magistrate if a dispensation is obtained. To get this dispensation you must follow the usual Catholic marriage procedures and offer a good reason for this special request. It is unwise to wait until the last minute to ask for this. It is not necessary for a priest to be present at such a ceremony.

The Church takes marriage very seriously. As a result, if you marry outside the Church without getting the necessary permissions, the marriage is not valid in the eyes of the Church.

This chapter has been so procedural that it may obscure something important: nearly everybody moves through the red tape without significant problems. And the end result is wonderful: a Christian marriage.

6. Buying a Bible

If you don't already own a good Bible, you certainly will want one. Getting the right version is not just a matter of walking into a bookstore and asking for a Bible. The clerk just might go to the back room, find one of a type that doesn't sell, blow off the dust and set you up for a big disappointment.

Bibles come in a variety of translations, covers, sizes, text papers and bindings. Some have many illustrations, often quite colorful. Some editions have expensive leather bindings and gilt-edged pages. The price may be unrelated to the quality of the translation.

If you are buying a Bible to put on display as a very visible symbol of the place of the word of God in a Christian home, maybe you will want one of the big, expensive editions complete with pages where you can record family births, deaths and marriages. But a book the size of an unabridged dictionary is not very readable. Set in your lap, the volume can cut off the circulation in your legs.

In selecting a Bible for regular use, your first decision is whether you want an old translation or a new one. The King James Bible is a classic of English literature; it is the traditional Bible of English-speaking Protestants. Some people are so used to its phrasing that they can't conceive of a Bible written in modern American English. If this is true of you, you might do

Don't you sell some
kind of abridged
Bible for beginners?

well to stay with the King James. Its quaint old-fash-
ioned language is beautiful. But remember that many
of the words and phrases have changed their meaning
since Shakespeare's time.

One thing is certain: you can do better than the
old Catholic version, the Douay. Its language is as
quaint as the King James though not quite so beautiful.
But its footnotes and explanatory materials are naïve
and lack the insights of recent Biblical scholarship. You
may also want to avoid the translations which came
out in the 1940s. The English is better, the explanatory
materials are better, but later translations have made
significant improvements over these. Catholic versions
of the 1940s Bibles are labeled (somewhere on the
flyleaf) "Confraternity" or "Knox."

Here is a good rule-of-thumb: Pick up a Bible
offered to you, open it, leaf through and try to find
the word "thou." If you can't find it, you're on the right
track. You are holding a Bible which has been enriched
by modern scholarship.

Another consideration is whether you want a Catholic or a Protestant version. Old fears of "slanting"
are now unfounded. The good modern translations are
reliable, whether they be Protestant or Catholic. There
are still a few sectarian versions circulating, but these
are conspicuously full of "thous" and archaic language.
You need not hesitate to purchase a modern Protestant
Bible if its language and format impress you.

Two differences still remain between Catholic and
Protestant versions. The Catholic list or "canon" of the
Old Testament books has several not usually found in
Protestant Bibles. These books are: Baruch, Judith,
Tobit (Tobias), Wisdom, Sirach (Ecclesiasticus), 1

and 2 Maccabees and the parts of Esther and Daniel originally written in Greek.

The other difference stems from the traditional Protestant emphasis on the Bible as the Word of God presented without comment or interpretation. Protestant Bibles often have no introductory materials. Footnotes usually refer only to possible variations in the original text. Catholic Bibles tend to have a wealth of introductory material and explanatory footnotes.

The Revised Standard Version is the most commonly used modern Protestant version. It is an honest effort to combine as much of the traditional phrasing as possible with the best of modern scholarship. Many Catholics prefer it for this reason. "Thou" is used only in those passages addressed to God. Some editions of the Revised Standard Version have the longer array of Old Testament books which they call "Apocrypha."

Other modern Protestant versions are now in circulation. The New English Bible is well done, but has a British accent to it. The Good News Bible published by the American Bible Society has a breezy American style. The Living Bible, an American paraphrase, though well written, departs too much from the original to merit consideration.

The two most commonly used modern Catholic Bibles are the Jerusalem Bible and the New American Bible. Both are in excellent modern English and both have abundant explanatory materials which reflect the best recent scholarship. The New American Bible's English is a bit clearer and easier to read, while the Jerusalem Bible's explanatory materials are better. The New American version is the one usually read at Mass.

One last consideration: what about the readability of the edition you propose to buy? Is the print crowded and small? Is the layout of pages a convenient and helpful one? Find an edition that does not weary the eye. Most Bibles come in a variety of editions. Reading a page or two will tell you if you have the right edition of the version that is best for you.

The written word of God can be an invaluable resource in your life. Whether or not access to that resource is convenient and pleasant will depend on how much care you put into choosing a Bible.

7. Visiting Churches

If you do much traveling or just plan to visit the different parishes of your diocese, you will find a surprising variety of Catholic churches. Some may be dark and quiet, some bare and bright, some heavy with big beams and massive columns, others hung with banners and simply constructed, some with the proportions of a pencil box, another with the surprises of a church in the round. You may come upon buildings as different as a church built by nineteenth century Lithuanian immigrants with many shrines, altars and statues, and a new suburban church which is angular and austere.

Church design is a matter of taste, and tastes change. But Catholic churches have many features in common. As a new Catholic you may have a special interest in recognizing the common features. So, let's consider some of the things you will find in most churches.

All Catholic churches make a distinction between the sanctuary, the area which includes the altar and lecterns, and the rest of the church. In Protestant usage the word "sanctuary" has a different meaning: it defines the whole church as distinguished from meeting rooms, kitchen, etc.

Many Catholic churches have a railing, called the Communion or sanctuary rail, which accentuates the separation of church sections. Every sanctuary has an altar. This is a table of wood, marble or stone standing in the center and apart from everything else. It should be the focal point of the whole church. The altar is covered, usually with white linen cloths. Liturgical reform calls for it to be kept uncluttered, even at Mass time.

In older churches you may find another altar, often of majestic dimensions, farther back, usually against the wall. This is the altar that was once used for the old Latin liturgy. Some people still call it the "main altar." If the tabernacle is on this altar, it may be used to reserve the Blessed Sacrament. In such circumstances, the old altar is called the "altar of repose" and the table altar is called the "altar of sacrifice."

Somewhere in the sanctuary there will be a prominent chair used by the priest at Mass when he is not busy at the lectern or altar. This chair is called the "president's chair" because the priest "presides" over the liturgy. Other chairs may be located beside it or elsewhere in the sanctuary. Those who assist at Mass use the side chairs.

Most churches have two lecterns in the sanctuary. Those who give the Scripture readings, the sermon, the announcements or comments and (sometimes) the Prayer of the Faithful stand at these lecterns. There may be an elevated speaker's box (called a pulpit) in lieu of one lectern. It is rare for anyone but the priest to use the pulpit.

Kneeling benches may be at the sides of the sanctuary or set in other convenient spots therein. These are usually portable and are called "prie-dieus," pronounced "pree-doo," from the French for "pray to

God." Prie-dieus are set out for the bridal couple at weddings.

To the left and right of the sanctuary area you usually will find side altars, the one on the left dedicated to Mary and displaying her statue, the one on the right dedicated to St. Joseph or the patron saint of the church. Large old churches may have even more altars along the left and right walls of the main part of the church. These altars rarely are used for Mass. They characteristically serve as shrines for private devotion. There may be boxes of candles placed nearby. An ancient custom is reflected here, and this is its symbolism: a person may want to spend a significant period of time in prayer but be unable to do so; so, he lights a candle and leaves it burning after he leaves to express this desire. A coin box is provided so that the cost of the candles may be covered by donations.

Of more universal significance is the tabernacle, where the Blessed Sacrament is reserved. The tabernacle is a solid metal box where consecrated hosts left over from Mass are kept. The consecrated wine is always consumed; it is never reserved in the tabernacle. In the days of the Latin liturgy, the tabernacle always was on the altar. You still may find it on the old altar, though many churches now have the tabernacle on one of the side altars or in a special place of its own.

The tabernacle is a favorite devotional spot. God is everywhere, and Jesus is found in our neighbors, but Catholics attach a very special significance to Christ's real presence in the consecrated hosts. So, many like to pray before the tabernacle. Often Catholics speak of "making a visit" to the Blessed Sacrament. A conspicuous candle, usually enclosed in red glass, is kept lighted as a reminder of Christ's special presence.

When you come from the sanctuary into the main part of the church, you will see little that is not found in a Protestant church. Of course, the confessionals are nearly a Catholic exclusive, but they are located inconspicuously at the sides or the back of the church. Stained glass windows are reminders of the days when most people couldn't read; in medieval times the scenes depicted there were the only Bible or catechism people had. Non-pictorial colored glass adds a bit of sacred atmosphere.

One distinctive note is the Stations of the Cross. You will notice fourteen numbered crosses along the walls. Often there is a picture or inscription or both accompanying each cross. This reflects a devotional practice dating back to the Crusades when Christians took risky pilgrimages to the Holy Land. In Jerusalem they could follow in the very footsteps of Jesus' last hours of life.

Under the influence of St. Francis of Assisi, fourteen crosses began to appear on the walls of churches, giving the faithful the opportunity to walk the same steps of Jesus, in mind and spirit, if not in body. The fourteen Stations recall specific events, proceeding from the moment Jesus was condemned to death by Pilate to the moment when he was taken down from the cross. Most of the events are mentioned in the Gospels. Some are legendary, such as the sixth Station, "Veronica wipes the face of Jesus." "Veronica" comes from the Greek for "true image."

Lent is a favorite time for this devotion. Usually it is done privately, with the person moving from Station to Station, praying and meditating on the incident recalled by the Station. Sometimes it is done as a church service, with the priest moving from Station to Station and the people remaining in their pews.

A last point of interest is the baptistry. This is usually located near the main doors of the church. It is there to symbolize the entrance of the newly baptized into the Church. The baptistry includes the baptismal font itself and the area around it.

Each church can have distinctive characteristics of its own, and the possibilities are too various to describe. Every diocese has one church which is considered the mother church of the diocese, the bishop's own church. This church is called the cathedral (from the Latin "cathedra"—chair; that is, the bishop's chair).

A church that is famous for its history or devotional appeal may be designated a "basilica." A chapel is a place other than a parish church where Mass can be offered regularly. A large church may have a small chapel as a separate part of the building.

Catholics have taken the liturgy everywhere. Masses in the home are not uncommon, and farm workers have had Masses in the fields. Nevertheless, you are likely to attend Mass most often in a church. This chapter will have served its purpose if it helps you to see the common characteristics shared by churches which may differ remarkably in design and decoration.

8. When Someone Is Sick

Jesus offered healing and forgiveness to those who came to him diseased or maimed in body or spirit. The Church continues this same ministry of healing and forgiveness through its clergy.

Priests visit parishioners who are chronically ill or invalids. The priest will hear a confession if the patient wants it and can bring Holy Communion on a regular schedule. Nevertheless, a priest is dependent on his parishioners to let him know who needs his services and to invite him to call. In cases of emergency, the priest will come at any hour of the day or night.

Emergency sick calls do not involve an elaborate ritual—despite anything misinformed Catholics or out-dated books may lead you to believe. For example, there is no need to meet the priest at the door with a lighted candle. In cases of emergency sick calls or the patient's reception of Holy Communion, it is necessary only to have a small table near the patient in clean and uncluttered condition. A fresh glass of water may prove helpful. The priest will bring everything else that is needed.

Priests also visit hospitalized parishioners. However, hospitals usually have a Catholic chaplain, a priest from a nearby parish, who brings the sacraments. Most hospitals ask the patient's religion and make the lists available to the clergy. Catholic priests often hesitate to visit non-Catholic patients unless they are specifically invited. The impression of imposing Catholicism on the sick is worth avoiding.

One of the problems a priest encounters when visiting a patient at home or in the hospital is the attitude of a patient who has been handled badly. Well-meaning relatives sometimes invite a priest to visit a patient who has been away from the sacraments for years and who has no intention of welcoming either the priest or the suggestion of confession. It makes good sense to inform the priest of the real situation so that he can act with sensitivity and understanding.

On his visits the priest is not concerned only with the sacraments of penance and Communion. He can encourage and console the patient and give him a chance to talk about his concerns. Ordinarily the priest will not bring Communion on the first visit. He will want to make sure that the patient is prepared for it. Pastors even have the right to confirm seriously ill parishioners who have missed the sacrament of confirmation.

But the sacrament most helpful to the seriously ill is the anointing of the sick (once called extreme unction). This sacrament has been the focus of superstition and myth. Its meaning can be distorted if there is a shortage of understanding among those concerned. The problem is a holdover from a time when anointing of the sick was widely considered to be the "last rites."

Anointing of the sick should not be considered an immediate preparation for death. So conceived, it may be postponed until the patient has been thoroughly drugged or is in a final coma. Relatives take great care not to frighten the patient. One result of this overprotectiveness can be that the patient loses most of the benefit of the sacrament. The anointing becomes little more than a farewell prayer to console the relatives.

According to the most serious teaching of the Church, the anointing of the sick is intended for anyone who is seriously ill. The Church recognizes the unity of the whole person, spiritual and physical, body and soul. One who is seriously ill may be despondent, feel useless or burdensome to others, feel abandoned by God. The anointing of the sick is intended to heal this spiritual disorder of illness and old age. The spiritual healing power of the sacrament sometimes helps a person to recover physically. Sins can be forgiven through the sacrament. The patient who receives it is in far better condition to face death, should it come.

It is hard to overemphasize the sadness of the game often played by the seriously ill patient and his relatives. The patient knows he is in a critical condition but pretends that he doesn't know so that his loved ones won't be alarmed. The relatives know his condition is critical but they pretend otherwise so that *he* won't be alarmed. And yet those who love the patient do not really want him deprived of the healing power of the sacrament. Love for the patient is best expressed by getting him spiritual help while he is conscious and capable of taking consolation.

As a new Catholic, you are not encumbered with common misunderstandings. If someone you love is ill or very old, you will want to talk to the person and help him to understand the real significance of the anointing. It is time to call the priest after such groundwork is done. It is good for the whole family to be present for the anointing, to join in the prayers and to be as much a part of it as possible.

Communion brought to the sick at the time of

anointing is called "viaticum." It would be ironic to note that "viaticum" means "food for the journey" if all Christian life were not considered a pilgrimage. This food may nourish further life. If death must come, it will nourish the person who must pass from this life to the next.

An enlightened Catholic will ask for the anointing when he is seriously ill. And he will take strength from it. Should it be necessary to face death, the sacrament will become an expression of Christian hope. "For if we believe that Jesus died and rose, God will bring forth with him from the dead those also who have fallen asleep believing in him" (I Thess. 4:14, NAB).

9. That First Year

Adjusting to a new Church is like adjusting to a new marriage: a lot depends on the individual and on the person's first experiences with the new institution. For some, the period of adjustment is challenging to say the least. For others, it is an easy, natural transition.

If you feel a bit challenged, you may find some general suggestions helpful. There is no ultimate wisdom in this chapter, but you will find simple recommendations based on varied experiences with many converts. You also will find a detour into discussion of confirmation: that is because the sacrament is one which converts often want access to early in their exploration of Catholic possibilities.

The first thing to pin down is this: what sort of adjustment are you facing? Those who become Catholics as adults are not a matched set. There are those who have been going to Mass for years, who are quite familiar with Catholic practices and folkways, and who already have some connection with a parish community. Then there are those who have hardly been to Mass at all, who find everything strange and different, and who wish that there were clearer road signs to guide the Catholic pilgrimage. From wherever you're starting, it will be wise to walk before you run.

If you don't know the simplest prayers like the

I didn't even know I'd
been a pagan until
somebody was rude
and brought it up today.

"Hail Mary," start there. Take time to get familiar with the sacraments. If you don't really understand basic doctrines, spend some time reading and trying to make some sense out of them. It may help to discuss troublesome points with informed Catholics or with a congenial priest. If you are already at home in a parish, any involvement with parish organizations should be limited to activities which seem particularly worthwhile to *you*. First enthusiasm is too good to waste on projects your heart is not in.

If the priest who instructed you is available, it might help to stop in and see him after a few months. He should be proud of his part in your religious adventure and undoubtedly will want to know how you are doing. Prior acquaintance with you may make him the right man to clear up misunderstandings, answer questions and help you feel at home in your new circumstances.

A sacrament you may have missed is confirmation. Current practice permits the priest-instructor to confirm the adults he receives into the Church. He doesn't have to confirm you, but he can. If you are confused about whether or not you received confirmation, your certificate of baptism or profession will clarify the matter. If you don't have the certificate, you can get a copy by asking the priest who received you or by writing to the place where your record is kept.

Confirmation ordinarily is administered by a bishop. If you weren't confirmed when you entered the Church, you probably will want to receive the sacrament before too long. The bishop usually makes the rounds of the parishes for confirmation, but in some places there is a confirmation for adults four times a year in the cathedral of the diocese.

The new rite of confirmation is impressive. Most of

your Catholic friends will have experienced a different rite and may not be too helpful in describing what to expect; so, some background follows here. The new rite recommends that you have as your sponsor the same person who sponsored you at baptism or at the profession of faith.

The ceremony emphasizes our dependence on the healing and strengthening power of the Holy Spirit. Confirmation preferably is celebrated in the context of a Mass in which the prayers call on the Holy Spirit to establish his enlivening presence in the persons to be confirmed.

After the reading of the Gospel and the homily, those to be confirmed renew their baptismal vows. The bishop extends his hands over the confirmands praying to the Holy Spirit to be their helper and guide, to give them the spirit of wisdom and understanding, the spirit of right judgment and courage, the spirit of knowledge and love, and the spirit of reverence in his service.

The bishop anoints each person individually with chrism, a special oil ·blessed on Holy Thursday. The sponsor places his hand on the candidate's right shoulder and gives the candidate's name to the bishop. (In some places the candidate gives his own name.) The bishop makes the sign of the cross with chrism on the person's forehead, saying (for example), "Mary, receive the seal of the Holy Spirit, the Gift of the Father." Mary responds, "Amen." The bishop says, "Peace be with you." Mary answers, "And also with you."

If you haven't received confirmation, it will be a renewing experience. It is a sign that you are a committed adult Christian ready to make your personal contribution to the community.

Turning to other aspects of your first year as a

Catholic, it is not overemphasis to repeat that the first year is a time to concentrate on your own personal religious needs. It is a time to overcome any awkwardness and to develop confidence in yourself in new roles. How long this initial period of adjustment should last depends on you and your own situation.

Yet, you may soon find that your personal growth depends on the support of the community. Few grow religiously by themselves, though holy hermits still turn up. Most Christians draw strength from their fellow Christians. As the community sustains you, you may feel compelled to return the favor. But the development of involvement should be natural, not a pressured transition.

Your contribution to parish life may be influenced by factors which include these two: (1) What are the parish's needs and priorities? (2) What talents and services are you equipped to contribute? High on nearly every parish's priority list is the religious education of parish children. But Christian concern should not be directed only to the young. You may ask yourself: is the continuing religious education of adults neglected? Are the old and the sick being cared for? What about the poor? If the neighborhood is changing racially, is the parish response the appropriate Christian response? How are the parish finances? Does the parish seem alive and active, or is it just a scattering of individuals who meet for Mass once a week?

When you have a grasp of the parish needs, you probably will want to find out who is doing something about them. The name of a parish organization is unimportant. The questions are: what people are effectively doing Christian work? What groups do they belong to? If such questions help you decide what group you want to work with, you can be forgiven if you don't want to rush in with a flaming sword and answers to everything. Churchgoers really need challenges, but the most effective work tends to be done by those who can work with imperfect people. Example works better than bare precept in the reform of parish organizations, experience seems to suggest. To avoid fighting inertia, start with a group that is accomplishing something. A group of determined somnambulists might be too much to cope with at first. A period of trial and error may be necessary before you find the best way to contribute your services.

Your perspective as a new Catholic and as a new parishioner can be particularly beneficial. By coming in with a fresh outlook and by raising new questions, you may help a group get out of its rut. As time goes on, you may find that you have leadership abilities. If not, simple competence in something you are suited to is contribution enough.

Your effort to give something of yourself to your parish community will be wasted only in parishes where community has died or never come alive. In a healthy parish, working with committed Christians can be an enlarging, enriching experience.

But don't rush in. Jesus assures us that "A man can have no greater love than to lay down his life for his friends." Nevertheless, your new friends in the parish have not been commissioned by God to kill your Christian enthusiasm by embroiling you in parish activities before you are ready for extensive involvement. For that first year, go at your own pace. The Christian enthusiasm you save may be your own.

10. Coping with Change

You know something about coping with change. You've just become a Catholic. That may have seemed like change enough for you. Maybe you expect to be a little disoriented for quite some time. This book has taken that for granted. But it also takes change in the Church for granted. This chapter suggests why you can expect the Church to undergo further change. If it leaves you reflecting on the concept, "Life means growth," it's not a wasted chapter.

By now you've met lifelong Catholics who are angry about "the changes." You've met those who are confused and disturbed by the same thing. You've met those who think that the Church has not changed enough. You may have been asked if you are for or against "the changes."

What kind of a question is that? After all, you may never have experienced an old Latin Solemn High Mass, leafed through a Baltimore catechism or eaten fish on Friday. Coming into the "new" Church, you escaped old hangups.

But you're familiar with problems resulting from change. You've given up old religious ways (or old non-religious ways), and maybe that wasn't easy. Your adjustment to Catholic liturgy, practices and folkways probably is still going on. You may know something of what the shaken Catholics are going through: you've taken a little shaking yourself.

It is good to sympathize with the shaken. It would be disastrous to fall into their kind of rut. Why raise this point? You've demonstrated your capacity for change. True, but what if some of the things you like best about the Church should change? Would you be terribly unsettled? To answer the question for yourself, consider how people get into religious ruts.

Generally people are not overly fond of change. Average people are average because they seek out a comfortable niche in which to be secure and happy. To be challenged or threatened is not sport for the average man or woman.

There are exceptions to this. Some changes are appreciated and looked forward to. We can hardly wait to graduate from school or to complete military service. We joyfully anticipate a wedding day or a promotion on the job. You yourself undoubtedly looked forward to the day when you became a Catholic. The happy changes may mean a bit of awkwardness and some demanding adjustments, but readiness for the stresses goes with the desire for change.

But change usually doesn't affect people this way. It is a jolt to see old familiar buildings razed. There's a song about having paradise replaced by a parking lot, and the message is not intended for the geriatric generation. Consider what usually happens when an old neighborhood absorbs a concentration of a new ethnic group. Who likes to see old friends pack up and move away to another state? If we have to move for the sake of a job, we may feel uneasy about "starting life all over."

In different degrees, resistance to change is built-in. We don't like to grow older, to develop chronic ailments, to have to slow down because the body isn't what it used to be. We certainly don't like to see loved ones die and pass out of our lives forever. Maybe we don't like to see a younger and different generation challenging our ideals and prejudices. Maybe we feel threatened by the challenge. Change can be unsettling.

If nothing else is an exception to our disinclination toward change, religion must be. God challenges us to become better, to do better. We remember the self-satisfied Pharisees of the Gospel story and the hard things Jesus said to them. If we don't want to be Pharisees, we won't be seeking a comfortable religious groove. But we are quite capable of settling for a routine of religious practices and a safe life-style that will guarantee us a contented life here and eternal happiness hereafter.

This is not to say that Catholicism is a swinging religion. To be a Catholic is to be a religious conservative in certain fundamental respects. The Church has survived 1,900 years, and we are still reciting ancient creeds. During all those centuries the Church has emphasized continuity and consistency with Jesus' teaching. This kind of conservatism was envisioned by Jesus. He expected the message carried by his disciples to be passed on through the centuries. We have felt the power of Jesus' teaching, and we want to pass on the real thing.

Then where does the trouble come in? It comes when Catholics fail to realize that their religion is like the mustard seed of the Gospel. "Another parable he put before them, saying: The Kingdom of heaven is like a grain of mustard seed which a man took and sowed in his field; it is the smallest of all seeds, but when it has grown it is the greatest of shrubs and becomes a tree, so that the birds of the air come and make nests in its branches" (Matt. 13: 31-32, RSV).

Christianity started out small, grew vast, and is still growing. Over the years cleansing rains and deadening snows have come and gone; the heat of fanaticism and the cold of dogmatism, the winds of reform, the receptive soil and the hard ground of indifference all have had their influence on growth. And birds of every variety have nested in the Church's branches.

But the Church remains rooted in Christ. Still, it is seen differently by different cultures, societies and civilizations. Religious practices and customs devised for one society have faded away as a new society developed. The language once used to express religious truth changed to express the same truth to different people.

The Church does experience periods of calm when things seem to have stabilized. If she settles for inertia, she stagnates. Turmoil, conflict, growth and decline have proved commoner than periods of calm. Change is normal.

What makes this particularly difficult for American Catholics to understand is their recollection of a long period of calm and stability. The quiet ended about 1960 with the election of President Kennedy and the coronation of Pope John XXIII. Change came with a rush, as it had throughout the Church's history.

Many Catholics had been led to believe that calm and stability were normal for the Church. Some Catholics saw the Catholic Church as a rock of security and serenity in a fast-deteriorating world. This view did not prepare people for the challenge, growth and conflict of the last decade.

This is your special concern only if you are unready for new challenges, growth and unrest. But consider whether or not your resiliency is sufficient. Institutions represent a sustaining continuity for those involved in them for years. Yet, as an institution changes, its people can find themselves involved with a different reality than the one which had made them feel at home. Made uncomfortable, people can look back on a more congenial time and romanticize it as a "golden age." The golden age usually is only one generation in the past; it is the province of those who live in memory, unwilling to meet the challenges of the present. "When I was a boy, things were better. . . ." Change from the folkways of twenty or thirty years ago is decline, a turning from the ideal.

Many Catholics romanticize the religious life of the 1940s or 1950s, especially since it was a period of calm and stability. As a new Catholic, you aren't likely to see the fifties or forties as a golden age. But if you are not conscious of the problem of the Catholic romanticizers, you eventually might set up the present time as your personal golden age. The period when you became a Catholic, when you struggled to understand, when you made your First Communion, when you first got the Church in perspective—this can become a time in Camelot, an unreal ideal.

Can you imagine yourself some years from now telling your children how beautiful the Catholic Church was in the 1970s? How you enjoyed a rich liturgy, how beautifully simple the sacraments were then, what great people were straightening out the parishes, how an insightful priest made the Church comprehensible to you. Could you find yourself lamenting the golden touch lost by a more callous generation of Catholics? Hopefully not.

The imaginable does not have to become real. Now is the time to realize that, though your present period of adjustment will end, you must continue to change and grow. Not every change is for the better, but change in the sense of growth is fundamental to Christianity.

You would not have become a Catholic if you didn't want to grow in love: love of God and love of your fellow human beings. Maturing, growing in knowledge and understanding, progress toward wisdom and perfect charity—these are the stuff of Christianity. Life means growth. So, live! And continue to grow.

Part II

"Have you understood all this?" They said to him, "Yes." And he said to them, "Therefore every scribe who has been trained for the kingdom of heaven is like a householder who brings out of his treasure what is new and what is old."—Matthew 13:51 (RSV)

The Catholic Church is a religious family with deep roots into the past. She lives in the present and looks to the future. We are not surprised that like the householder in the Gospel she constantly brings out of her treasure the old and the new. In this second part of the book we look first at the old—the ways that have been with us for a long time and still remain with us. Some of these ways are fading, some show extraordinary resiliency. We will then look at the new—whether they are the ways of the future or ways that are destined to pass quickly, time will tell. They are with us now.

"Every day's a holy day with me...."

11. Liturgical Life

The everyday calendar is uneventful: it's a long time between holidays. On the other hand, the Church calendar is full of people (saints), events (holy days) and liturgical moods (seasons). Each day is dedicated to some saint, but this is not the place to learn about three or four hundred religious heroes. The important thing is the heart of the liturgical calendar, celebration of the life, death and resurrection of Jesus. Following the biblical path of Jesus throughout the year, the liturgy keeps Catholics aware of Jesus' words and purposes. The liturgy will make new sense to you if you understand its cycles.

The Church year begins with the season of *Advent,* a period of four weeks which ends with Christmas. The Advent season commemorates the long wait of mankind for its Redeemer, the turbulent history of the Chosen People, especially its prophets, and the role of John the Baptist as the immediate forerunner of Jesus. The mood of Advent is sober but not grim because there is an undercurrent of joyful expectation.

Christmas ushers in a season of joy and hope. During this season the Church commemorates the childhood, public appearance (Epiphany) and baptism of Jesus. The Christmas season lasts just two to three weeks.

The next few weeks have no special significance. The Sundays of this period are simply numbered (for example, Third Sunday of the Year).

Lent is the most distinctive season of the Church's year. It begins on *Ash Wednesday* in the seventh week before Easter. The date of Easter varies. Since Easter is the focal point of the Church's year, the dates of most significant celebrations vary with it. Lent is thought of as a forty-day period. It is, if you don't count Sundays.

On Ash Wednesday Catholics customarily come to church to receive ashes. The distribution of ashes usually takes place at Mass. The priest places the ashes on the recipient's forehead in the form of a cross, saying, "Remember, man, that you are dust and unto dust you shall return" or, "Repent and believe the Good News." This sobering ceremony sets the tone for the season of Lent.

Lent is a time for consciousness of sin, a season of repentence and personal renewal. It commemorates the last dark months of Jesus' life when his popular following drifted away and his enemies plotted his downfall. The mood of Lent is serious but not morbid.

On the Fridays of Lent, Catholics are expected to observe the traditional abstinence from meat. Ash Wednesday and Good Friday are days of fasting as well as abstinence. Fasting limits the day's meals to one full meal and two half meals. In acknowledgement of the penitential spirit of Lent, it is customary for Catholics to do something extra or give up something throughout the season. Some give extra attention to service to others; some make much of giving up sweets; what is done is an individual thing, but the current emphasis is on positive Christian actions. Of course, Lent is an appropriate time for the sacrament of penance.

The final week of Lent is the most solemn of the year. It begins with Palm Sunday, the traditional name being just that despite all efforts of liturgical experts to get it changed. On this day palms are blessed in the parishes and distributed to the people. Sometimes there is a procession. The symbolism ties in to the brief triumphal entry of Jesus into Jerusalem, when palm leaves were spread in his path. At Mass the Passion is read ("Passion" is from the Latin "passio," meaning suffering, endurance). This is the Gospel account of the suffering, crucifixion and death of Jesus. Sometimes the Passion is read by three readers, with the congregation speaking some of the lines.

This final week of Lent is called Holy Week. On Holy Thursday, a special Mass commemorating the Last Supper and the institution of the Eucharist is celebrated. On Good Friday there is no Mass. A "Liturgical Action" takes its place. It includes another reading of the Passion, the veneration of the cross and Holy Communion.

The mood changes abruptly at the Easter Vigil, celebrated late on Holy Saturday. The church is in darkness, a flame is started, the Paschal Candle lit and the light passed from person to person. This movement from darkness to light, from sadness to joy, symbolizes the victory of Jesus over death by his resurrection. The ceremony is long and includes many readings and a baptismal liturgy and concludes with the first jubilant Mass of Easter. This celebration of the resurrection is the high point of the liturgical year.

Easter Sunday begins a season of triumph and gladness, of awareness of forgiveness, salvation and the pledge of eternal life. The Easter season lasts for seven weeks. On the fortieth day after Easter, called Ascen-

sion Thursday, there is a special celebration of the
return of the risen Jesus to his Father. The Easter season concludes with Pentecost Sunday, a commemora-
tion of the Holy Spirit's coming to the first Christians,
an event which inspired them to preach the good news
to the whole world.

From Pentecost until the following Advent, there
are no major liturgical happenings. The Sundays are
numbered and continue the enumeration from before
Lent (for example, Fifteenth Sunday of the Year).

Scattered throughout the year are special commem-
orations of events in the life of Jesus, Mary and some
of the saints. These are called "feasts." Examples are
the feast of the Annunciation on March 25 and the
feast of St. Francis of Assisi on October 4. The most
significant feasts are called holy days. Catholics are
expected to attend Mass on these days, which vary
somewhat from country to country. The holy days
celebrated in the United States are:

Immaculate Conception (December 8)
Christmas
New Year's
Ascension Thursday
Assumption of Mary (August 15)
All Saints (November 1)

The liturgical colors used on the altar vary with the
season of the liturgical year or the feast celebrated.
This is most noticeable in the color of the Mass vest-
ments. White is used for the Christmas and Easter seasons and for feasts of Jesus, Mary and most saints.
Purple is used in Advent and Lent. Red is used on Palm
Sunday, Good Friday, Pentecost and on feasts of mar-
tyred saints (who shed their blood for the faith). Green

is used at any other time. Purple or white is used at funerals and white is used at weddings.

Considered all at once, the liturgical cycle seems very complicated. As it is experienced, the cycle will become coherent and simple enough. If you live the liturgical year—share the Church's consciousness of the aspects of Jesus' life celebrated from season to season—you will find yourself naturally oriented toward the life of Jesus and its implications for you.

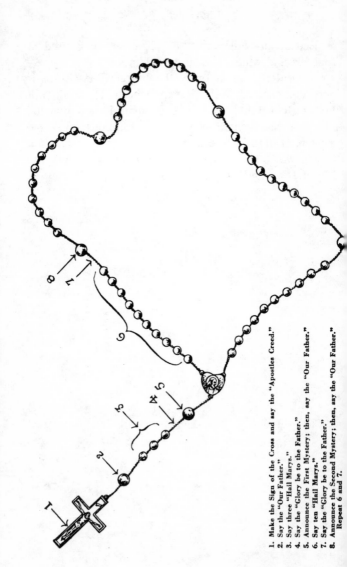

1. Make the Sign of the Cross and say the "Apostles Creed."
2. Say the "Our Father."
3. Say three "Hail Marys."
4. Say the "Glory be to the Father."
5. Announce the First Mystery; then, say the "Our Father."
6. Say ten "Hail Marys."
7. Say the "Glory be to the Father."
8. Announce the Second Mystery; then, say the "Our Father."
   Repeat 6 and 7.

12. Devotional and Prayer Life

Eucharistic Devotions

The Eucharist is the great essential for Catholics, and its usual setting is the Mass. The simplification of the Mass has placed the Eucharist even more firmly in its natural context. Consequently, the popularity of separate eucharistic devotions has tended to wane somewhat. Nevertheless, many Catholics still find great significance in visits to the Blessed Sacrament reserved in the tabernacle.

Special eucharistic observances are common. There is the custom of receiving Communion on the first Friday of the month. There is the special eucharistic service called "Benediction of the Blessed Sacrament." In this service the priest takes the large consecrated host from the tabernacle, puts it in a large display vessel called a "monstrance" and sets the monstrance on the altar. Hymns are sung, incense is offered and prayers are recited. Toward the end of the service, the priest blesses the people with the host in the monstrance.

Liturgical changes allowing Mass in the evening have made the Benediction service less prevalent. In some churches, on certain days, the Blessed Sacrament is still "exposed" in the monstrance on the altar for public veneration. Sometimes this is done once a year for a period of forty hours. The Forty Hours devotion has an opening and a closing ceremony, and during the intervening time various groups keep a vigil in the Church. It is the custom to genuflect on both knees when the Blessed Sacrament is exposed. In some predominantly Catholic countries, the feast of Corpus Christi in June is the occasion for a public procession with the Blessed Sacrament.

Marian Devotions

Next to the Eucharist, devotion to Mary is most popular among Catholics. Most of the medals and cloth badges called "scapulars" that are worn are related to Mary in some way. Some churches have devotional services in honor of Mary. These may run for a period of nine days and are called "novenas." Often such services are held on the same day of the week throughout the year and are called "perpetual novenas." May and October are favorite months for Marian devotions. Sometimes a novena is held in honor of the Holy Spirit or one of the saints.

The *rosary* is the most popular of Marian devotions. Though it may seem dull and repetitious to new Catholics, it need not be if the pattern of meditation on the "mysteries" (events in the lives of Jesus and Mary) is followed. If you are interested, find a book or leaflet that will explain this pattern to you.

To say the rosary, this is what you do. On the crucifix say the Apostles' Creed. On the large or isolated bead say the Our Father; on the next three beads say a Hail Mary. On the final bead say the Glory Be. The rest of the rosary is divided into five clusters of ten beads called "decades." For each decade, say the Our

Father once, the Hail Mary ten times and the Glory Be once. Most born Catholics will be happy to demonstrate this for you.

Retreats

Most Protestant churches have some kind of spiritual renewal activity periodically. It may be as fundamental as a revival or as sophisticated as a group encounter. Among Catholic activities aimed at spiritual renewal, two stand out: "retreats" and "missions." For a retreat, a group of people gathers at a place removed from the workaday scene. During a mission, a priest or group of priests comes into a parish for a week or two.

Scattered throughout a diocese, often at the edge of a metropolitan area, there are "retreat houses." They are usually operated by religious orders. A group of people with some common bond—sometimes they are all teen-agers, sometimes single men or women, sometimes married couples, often members of the same parish organization—meet at a retreat house. Usually this is for a weekend—Friday evening to Sunday afternoon—but a retreat can be longer or shorter than that.

The program includes talks by a priest or other qualified people, group discussion, and opportunities for prayer, meditation, confession, counseling or just walking in the woods. Room and board are provided for a modest fee. It is a chance for people to get away for some serious thinking and praying.

Missions

A mission is quite different. Its purpose is to revitalize a parish, to renew individual commitment and to get indifferent Catholics motivated toward the sacramental life. The traditional pattern calls for a service in church every night with a long sermon and confessions afterward. The week ends in a final service on Sunday afternoon with a special mission blessing. There are separate weeks for men and women (the women's week comes first, and the missionaries often urge the ladies to recruit the men for the following week's services) with afternoon services for school children.

Television and fear of going out at night have affected turnouts. Alternate forms of missions have been tried. Home Masses in each section of the parish, neighborhood discussions over coffee, special events for parish organizations, etc., are means used to keep the mission alive. The missionaries usually belong to religious orders which specialize in this work.

Of course, the word "mission" has other meanings. There are missionaries in foreign countries working for the spread of Christianity, and in this country a church without a resident priest is called a mission. But these usages are beside the point at hand.

Devotional and prayer life are an individual matter. The Mass is the shared essential. How you pray and express devotion outside of the Mass is entirely up to your own needs and preferences.

13. Organizations

Some old parish organizations are perishing, and new organizations are cropping up. The more durable of the established organizations merit a brief comment.

There are still catchall men's and women's organizations. For the men there is the *Holy Name Society.* A monthly Communion Sunday and a breakfast meeting featuring a football coach or other non-controversial type may be all that bind the group together. For the women there may be something like the *Altar and Rosary Society.* Sometimes this is just a small group of women who concentrate on care of the sanctuary.

In some parishes you will find the *Legion of Mary.* Always a small group, the Legion blends Marian devotion with zealous efforts to get "fallenaways" back to Mass and the sacraments. Most parishes have a *St. Vincent de Paul Society* which provides a temporary aid to the needy of the parish.

The letters *CCD* do not designate a federal agency. They refer to the Confraternity of Christian Doctrine. The CCD is an effort to provide Catholic religious education for children who go to public schools. Men and women from the parish serve as teachers, preferably after training by professionals.

The letters *CFM* stand for the Christian Family Movement. The CFM is an organization of married couples who meet in homes in groups of five to eight

Join the Ladies' Guild?
That sounds like a union
for
guilded women!

couples. The groups discuss Scripture, liturgy and the problems of the neighborhood and the wider community. Following a format of "see, judge and act," the groups try to move from discussion to concrete action.

The *Knights of Columbus* is a men's society organized into "councils" which draw their membership from an area larger than that of a parish. The Knights were originally organized as an insurance society and as a sort of Catholic counterweight to the Masons. Frequently criticized as being little more than a social club, the Knights in many places do effective Christian work.

In many colleges and universities, state or private, there is an organization of Catholic students called the Newman Club. The club has officers, survives (hopefully) on dues (but not usually), and sponsors a variety of religious, intellectual, social and social action programs.

An earlier comment bears repetition at this point: in healthy parishes, the Christian work gets done by people organized into groups which may have traditional names or new names. The important question is: which organizations have their Christian priorities straight? These are the groups which are worth a new Catholic's time. You can afford to avoid the rest.

14. Social Customs

The Wake

The most distinctive American Catholic social custom is the wake. It grew up originally in Ireland where the time of bereavement was one of the few occasions when the British authorities would allow the natives to gather in large numbers. Though the days of great celebration with drinking and conversation to the wee hours of the morning may be over, the wake is still an important part of American Catholic social life. The custom is not confined to the Irish; it is popular with most ethnic Catholic groups.

It starts with the obituary listings in the newspaper —one newspaper. Catholics always use one particular newspaper for their obituaries; any older Catholic will tell you which one it is. Catholics scan the obituary columns to see if a relative or friend or old neighborhood acquaintance has died. They note carefully the funeral parlor and the visiting hours, and make their plans accordingly. In some large families, one or two of the older women may have this task and take it upon themselves to notify all the relatives.

Wakes are more than a homage to the dead person. They are great gatherings of the clan. Relatives who have not seen or talked to each other for years show up at a wake. As a new Catholic unfamiliar with this custom, you may hesitate to get involved. But if you are married to a born Catholic, you will find no better way to be accepted into the family. Failure to attend a wake will be carefully noted and rarely forgiven.

At the wake, you and your children will be closely inspected by maiden aunts and second cousins. I say your children—you can leave the little ones at home, but children of ten or older are expected to attend and meet the members of the clan. When you are new to the family, an older relative will take charge of you and introduce you to all the family members. You do not have to meet the friends and neighbors unless they happen to be talking to a relative.

The procedure is this: when you enter the funeral parlor, make sure you go to the right room. Enter the room, smile and nod but do not try to meet anyone unless another person makes the first move. Go to the front of the room toward the casket. Standing close to the casket are the closest relatives of the deceased. Wait your turn, introduce yourself if you have to, and express your condolences.

Then wait your turn if necessary and kneel down at the casket and pray for the deceased. Afterwards, another word or two to a close relative is appropriate unless the line of visitors is long. Then look around for someone you know. If you don't know anyone, a more distant relative will recognize your plight and take you in tow. From then on, it's a matter of meeting the other relatives until you have made the rounds.

On one night of the wake, about 8:00, a priest comes in and leads the rosary or one of the newer wake services. It is bad form to duck out when this begins. It is equally bad form to arrive so late at the wake that the immediate relatives of the deceased are detained. They are not enjoying the wake as much as the others are. If you have arranged for a Mass to be offered for the deceased, place the card on the table provided for that purpose. Be sure to sign the register; it is proof that you were there.

Bingo

Legends of fabulous wealth to the contrary, most Catholic organizations are perennially short of money. A variety of fund-raising devices are used to alleviate the problem. Some of them you are familiar with—bazaars, bake sales, used book sales. You may feel a bit uneasy about some of the other methods used—raffles and the weekly bingo games—especially when they are against the law.

The origins of bingo are hard to trace historically. It quickly became popular among American Catholics. The number of schools built and parishes enabled to survive through bingo must be in the thousands. The game is most popular among older women, but you may find reluctant husbands there too. It is now fashionable among "liberated" Catholics to express contempt for bingo. You can do this if you want, but try not to be too self-righteous about it or you will make enemies.

Perhaps a word of explanation about the strong difference of feeling between white Protestants and ethnic Catholics on gambling is in order here. Most American Protestants and many upper class Catholics have accepted what has been called the Protestant ethic. This is the American ethic of thrift and hard work, with the underlying conviction that it is a sin to receive a

monetary or material gain that you have not earned or in-
herited. Most Catholics and some other Americans hold
to the medieval ethic—God is the true owner of all property; what we possess is on loan from him. Therefore
an unexpected bonanza is a gift of God and should be
received and enjoyed gratefully.

Wearing a religious
habit has some
compensations.

15. Religious Orders

The variety of Catholic religious orders reflects the diversity of Christian apostolic concerns. Religious orders or communities have sprung up at every stage in the Church's history to meet special needs or crises. The orders are not immune to social pressures, and with time and social change they often become quite different from what their founders intended.

Historically, religious orders began simply. A group of men or women, usually with a forceful leader, felt a need for spiritual growth and closer union with God. They decided to live together and to accept Jesus' invitation to a life of poverty (Matt. 19: 16-22) and chastity (Matt. 19: 10-12). They agreed to accept a rule of life and the governance of superior officials, vowing obedience. Often they chose a special task as the work of the order.

If the group or "order" survived initial difficulties, achieved stability and attracted new members, the order might request to have itself approved and recommended by Rome. A distinctive mode of dress might be adopted, called a "habit." If the order grew and expanded into new countries, it might make changes in its life-style and work.

The oldest order in the Church which has survived to the present day is the Benedictines (sixth century). In the United States there are about 120 orders of men and 400 of women.

Religious orders function as independent entities in the Church. Though subject to Rome, they have their own government, which can be quite democratic. A few small groups are subject to a bishop, but the great majority are independent of the diocesan or parish authority. They make their own arrangements with a bishop or pastor for their services.

Every order has its official title, which may be wordy, and most have a popular nickname. The order to which this author belongs, for example, is officially known as "The Society of Missionary Priests of St. Paul the Apostle." Its nickname is the "Paulists." Members of an order carry a set of initials after their names to identify them by order. The initials can be different from those of the official title or nickname—"C.S.P.," from the Latin "Congregatio Sancti Pauli," are the initials of the Paulist order.

Some religious orders of men are composed entirely of priests and those studying for the priesthood. Others have no priests at all; members are called "Brothers." Some orders have both priests and brothers. "Monk" is an old term applied to members of certain orders such as the Franciscans. A monk can be either a priest or a brother.

Members of women's orders are called "sisters" or "nuns" or "religious." At the present time, the designations are used interchangeably. In the United States sisters have been the main force behind the success of the Catholic schools, but teaching is only one of many specialties pursued by women religious.

More frequently than men's orders, the women's communities get gratuitous advice on how to live their lives. Those who want nuns "to dress like nuns" forget that the traditional habits were originally an adaptation of the costume commonly worn by women at the time the order began.

About 35% of the priests in the United States are members of religious orders. The other 65% are directly responsible to the various dioceses and are called "diocesan" or "secular" priests. The diocesan priests do the bulk of the parish and administrative work of the Church. "Religious" priests are more likely to do teaching or some specialized work. Some religious orders have affiliated organizations for lay people, which are sometimes called "Third Orders."

The variety of existing religious orders suggests that Catholic unity is not achieved at the expense of individuality. In a small diocese like Grand Rapids, for example, religious orders are active in many fields. Conventual Franciscans give parish missions. The Consolata Fathers operate two centers for the inner city poor and a parish for ethnic Italians. Dominicans provide a theology faculty for a Catholic college and a campus chaplain for state colleges. Franciscans do parish missions and staff parishes. The Oblates of Mary Immaculate staff a parish and a hospital chaplaincy. Paulists run a Catholic Information Center and a downtown chapel. Redemptorists staff a parish, do parish missions and hospital work, while Vincentians maintain a retreat house. Of course diocesan priests dominate the parochial ministry and do many other things, but a glimpse at the variety of religious orders and their work suggests the diversity present in Catholic unity.

"What is new. . . ."

16. Movements

Beginning in the early 1960s and under the influence of the Second Vatican Council, a variety of "movements" have stirred the American Catholic Church. Thanks to Eric Hoffer's study, *The True Believer,* a careful writer is not comfortable identifying anything he likes as a mass movement. But like it or not, there have been developments in the Church which can best be described as movements. As used here, the term "movement" describes a new emphasis which starts with small groups, attracts people widely, and gradually acquires some sort of national structure to promote it.

Most American Catholics may avoid the movements, but they have considerable influence and sometimes have impact enough to draw strong opposition from Catholic clergy and people. Though most of the movements have been accused of being radical, their representatives tend to trace their inspiration to the Second Vatican Council. Movement members usually are orthodox in theology but sometimes unconventional in their activities.

The Cursillo

The earliest of the contemporary Catholic movements is the Cursillo, pronounced "cur-see-yo," meaning "little course." It started in Spain as an effort to instill a strong Christian commitment in Spanish men. The cursillo was introduced into the United States in Texas and has been adapted to American tastes.

The focus of the movement is the three-day cursillo, an intense retreat which demands more than the conventional retreat. You must be invited to make a cursillo, and participants must have a letter of recommendation from their pastor. The aim is to attract leaders. Wives may be invited to make a cursillo later, but the men must become "cursillistas" first.

The cursillo itself lasts from Thursday evening until Sunday afternoon. It differs from the ordinary retreat which tends to be relaxed and to place the emphasis on individualism. The rector (lay leader) and his team possess the recommendations and evaluations of each man's pastor and sponsor. Through intense group dynamics they try to draw out a man's strengths and make him face up to his weaknesses.

The cursillo program includes fifteen talks and five meditations. Thursday evening is spent in a quiet examination of conscience. Friday is devoted to knowledge of self: who am I? Saturday is spent in coming to know Christ: who is Christ? Coming to know Christ in our neighbor is Sunday's theme. The program is avowedly Catholic and heavily sacramental.

The cursillo does not end on Sunday afternoon. It is understood beforehand that participants have made a commitment to what is called the "fourth day." They are expected to attend the large group meetings called "ultreya" and smaller meetings of four or five people. Through sharing and mutual reinforcement, cursillistas are motivated toward piety, study and action. Cursillistas are expected to work to Christianize the environment they work and live in.

The Catholic Pentecostals

Cursillistas sometimes drift into the Pentecostal movement, but they are not its main inspiration. Catholic Pentecostalism is adapted from Protestant Pentecostalism. For generations in America, fundamentalist or "third force" churches like the Assembly of God or the Church of God (of Cleveland, Tennessee) have been proclaiming a new Pentecost in which the dramatic manifestations of the Holy Spirit described in the New Testament have reappeared in our time. Catholics traditionally have not had a brotherly feeling toward Pentecostals, but in the 1960s some Catholics began to see Pentecostalism differently.

They studied the Pentecostals with friendly interest and began to hold small prayer meetings. Soon the charismatic gifts appeared to surface among them. Catholics began to pray in tongues, speak prophecies and interpret them and claimed to experience miracles of spiritual and, at times, physical healing.

The movement has grown rapidly and has strong centers at the Universities of Notre Dame and Michigan. It has spread to many areas of the American heartland. It is weakest on the East and West coasts. Members of the movement accept the term "Pentecostal" but prefer to think of themselves as involved in "Charismatic Renewal."

The weekly prayer meeting is the heart of the Pentecostal movement. The meetings may be quite small, but often they include hundreds of people. Persons of all ages and backgrounds attend the prayer meetings. Protestants are welcomed. There is much spontaneity, but the leader is expected to maintain a careful control. Unruly elements are not welcomed, and attacks against Catholic doctrine or Church authority are met with a stony silence.

The meetings include singing of hymns, readings from the Bible, personal testimonies to the work of the Spirit in one's life, admonitions to a close personal relationship with Jesus, spontaneous prayers and requests for prayers for various intentions. Catholic Pentecostals have been charged with everything from mass hysteria to orgiastic worship. This seems to be a harsh, maybe even near-hysterical reaction.

Genuinely controversial are the extraordinary manifestations of the Holy Spirit. These include praying in tongues, prophecies, and interpretations of prophecies. Praying in tongues begins with expressions of praise in English in low voices from all parts of the room. Someone then begins singing in strange syllables and others join in. It often has a hauntingly beautiful sound, rises in crescendo and then falls.

Prophecies are spoken by one or more individuals in a strange tongue. They are interpreted by other individuals. The interpretations are usually admonitions to prayer and repentance, to acceptance of Jesus and openness to the Spirit. Pentecostals are convinced that the tongues and prophecies are spoken in some real ancient or modern language unknown to the speaker, under the direct influence of the Holy Spirit. To others they sound like random syllables of Hebrew or Greek.

A Pentecostal community usually has a recognized leader, a small pastoral team and a larger core group. These people may have a smaller prayer meeting at a different time than the general meeting.

Among those who attend the large weekly meetings there are many who drift in and out of the movement, some motivated by curiosity, some by an enthusiasm which wanes. Sometimes classes are held to explain the movement to newcomers.

Most clergy are suspicious of the Pentecostal upsurge. But some nuns, priests and brothers have become enthusiastic supporters. The durability of the movement will be tested in the next decade.

The Campus Ministry

The present campus ministry has its roots in the old Newman movement. The older movement dates back two or three generations and attempted to do three things for Catholic students on secular college campuses:

1. provide a sanctuary for religious practice and a citadel of orthodoxy in the secular environment;

2. provide a social club for Catholic students and increase the prospects for Catholic marriages; and

3. serve as "Catholic schools on campus" where Catholic students could take courses in philosophy and theology of a quality equal to academic courses offered at the college.

This was a defensive posture, and it changed, particularly with the beginning of the civil rights movement. Catholic chaplains and students began to join Protestants, Jews and secular liberals in espousing the cause of blacks. It was not the first American Catholic venture into activism, but it came when such a venture was unexpected. It changed the role of the campus ministry and its effects spilled over into the Church at large.

Soon cooperative efforts on campus sent clergy and students of all faiths into the South for protest marches and into the Northern slums for tutoring and community action projects. Other minority groups were recognized and many social injustices began to be called by their right names. The student passivity of the 1950s yielded to the activism of the 1960s, and not without religious leadership. Students of an activist temperament began to crowd tamer students out of the religious centers, to the delight of the chaplains.

At Catholic campus centers, sisters, faculty and professional people formed teams to lead the students to develop mature Christian attitudes and to commit themselves to the struggle for racial and social justice. As time went on, the Vietnam war drew out anti-war activism and encouraged hostility to the military-industrial establishment.

Upheaval did not always produce mature Christians. Some activists abandoned the Church altogether. The focus on activism brought a spiritual vacuum to some others, and students were found complaining that their religious needs were being neglected. A new student interest in mysticism, meditation and magic grew up apart from the religious centers and their activist leadership.

The campus ministry has tended to reevaluate responsibilities and today provides a balance between religious reinforcement and social involvement.

The Catholic Left

Just as cursillistas sometimes become Pentecostals,

campus activists sometimes move to the Catholic Left.
The Catholic Left is the most controversial of all the
movements. It appeared on the scene suddenly. Most
Catholics were unprepared for the new phenomenon.
It seemed to contradict the prevailing ethos of American Catholicism, though this was precisely where it had
its roots.

American Catholics characteristically have been
strongly patriotic. As a minority in a largely Protestant
country, Catholics were more apt to volunteer for its
wars, became enthusiastic flag wavers and often were
less critical of national institutions and policies. The
aftermath of World War II, when the Soviet Union
imposed its rule on Catholic Eastern Europe, stimulated
a strong anti-Communist strain which reinforced traditional patriotism. There seemed to be little possibility
of a Catholic Left.

But American Catholics had retained an awareness
of what it meant to be a persecuted minority. Though
too many were not happy to have blacks move into their
neighborhood, others felt instinctively that the minority
suffered at the hands of an unfair majority. Some developed early sympathy for people of color who fought
bravely against a super-power.

For generations, too, the American Catholic pulpit
and press had thundered against secularism and mate-
rialism. The people were told Sunday after Sunday that
money and success in the system were not the highest
values. The surprise came when some Catholics began
to take these themes as calls to action.

Coming from the campus ministry, the civil rights
movement and the peace movement and strong in the
conviction that American society is corrupt and ma-
terialistic, small groups of Catholics and others organ-

ized to fight the establishment and to end the Vietnam war.

Repudiating the violence of SDS and other militant New Left groups, they protested by burning draft cards, encouraging conscientious objection, and supporting the neglected—everybody from welfare mothers to Chicano grape pickers. At the border between violence and non-violence, a few raided draft boards and destroyed records.

At the end of the Vietnam war, the Catholic Left lost its focus. Some have become interested in the Third World countries and follow the "liberation theology" of Latin America, a blend of Catholicism and Marxism. Others have become concerned with the rights of women and other groups in the Church. "Divorced Catholics" has many local groups across the country; it provides emotional support and counseling for divorced people and often agitates for change in the Church's marriage legislation. "Dignity" functions in somewhat the same way for Catholic homosexuals. However Catholics may respond to all this, it keeps us from being complacent.

17. In the Parishes

Parish Councils

Phylis McGinley wrote a little poem about the old prelate who half forgot whether he was custodian or master of God's House. Before Vatican II it was easy for a pastor to feel very masterful. He ran the parish with a little help from his friends. Sometimes the assistant priests got to help, too. Since Vatican II the assistants have in some places risen to the status of "associate pastors," and sometimes the title is not empty. Through parish councils laymen have gained the opportunity to affect parish policy and programs, too—but not everywhere.

The parish councils, elected by the parishioners, are designed to establish an official lay structure for the parish. They usually have a governing board and a number of committees responsible for finances, administration of parish property, the parochial school, the religious education of public school children, social service, the liturgy and ecumenism.

Sometimes sisters and priests serve on the parish council. Whether or not the councils work out depends on factors as variable as the pastor's openness, the individual council member's competence, the readiness of the parish community for constructive innovation, the influence of the old guard, etc.

In some places the councils have real responsibility and authority. In others they are simply advisory boards which can be managed or ignored by the pastor. The potential of the councils is immense. They can be a major factor in the development of a responsible laity.

Deacons

Though deacons are a new phenomenon in the parishes, the diaconate is actually an ancient order in the Church, the third level of the Sacrament of Holy Orders (after bishop and priest). Very important in the early Church, the diaconate was allowed to decline into a mere stepping-stone on the way to the priesthood.

The Sacrament of Holy Orders gives deacons the right to preach, to baptize, to distribute Holy Communion, and to officiate at marriages and funerals. They cannot celebrate the Eucharist, forgive sins or anoint the sick. These sacramental functions are reserved to the priests.

There are two kinds of deacons. There are those who are preparing to become priests and have vowed celibacy. They are ordained to the diaconate a year or so before being ordained priests. Formerly confined to seminary studies for that year, they are now being assigned to parishes as a sort of apprenticeship. They live in the rectory and do a variety of parish tasks.

Less familiar to Catholics is the diaconate of mature married men authorized by the Second Vatican Council. Convinced Catholics who have achieved a proper level of responsibility in their business or professional lives and who have stable marriages can be selected for the diaconate. They are trained for two years in theology and pastoral practice and then ordained as deacons. What their role will be in the parishes will have to be determined by themselves primarily, with the cooperation of the priests and parishioners.

Liturgical Roles

It took remarkable liturgical changes to bring you many of the common features of today's Mass. The *lector* reads the first two passages from the Bible. The *commentator* sets the theme for the Mass, comments at different times and gives certain directions. The *leader of song* leads the singing, but before Vatican II his counterpart was confined to the choir. The roles of *server* (or altar boy), organist or musicians and choir are not new.

Often one person fills a variety of these roles. Catholic men may be invited to fill any of these roles, but getting women on the altar is difficult in some places.

A ceremony of investiture is required before a person becomes an authorized *minister of the Eucharist*. This is a new role for lay people. In some dioceses women can take this assignment and distribute Communion, and their service in this role is probably an indicator of the future.

Baptism of Babies

There is one significant change in the new rite for baptism of infants: the parents take a prominent role, while the role of godparents is diminished. In the ceremony of the past, the priest addressed the child as if he were an adult, and the godparents answered for the child. In the new rite the priest questions the parents and godparents about their own faith and their intention to raise the child in the Catholic faith.

Baptism is done in the church, usually on Sundays. It is still expected that the godparents be Catholic and that the child will be given a saint's name, though there are exceptions to this. Shortly after a child is born, you can contact the local priest and find out what is expected of you as a parent and what arrangements have to be made for baptism. In emergency cases, a child may be baptized without ceremony. And you, as a Christian, can do it.

This is a good note on which to end. It reminds us that individual Christians have great power: we are a "royal priesthood" (the words are St. Peter's), a People of God commissioned collectively and individually to do Jesus' work. Each Christian—priest, religious or lay person—shares in this opportunity. So, if you delight in your recent baptism or profession of faith, that is good and right. Brotherhood with Jesus is no small privilege; and to do his work, no small joy.

Appendix

SOME COMMON PRAYERS

The Sign of the Cross

In the name of the Father, and of the Son, and of the Holy Spirit. Amen.

The Our Father (traditional version)

Our Father, who art in heaven, hallowed be thy name; thy kingdom come; thy will be done on earth as it is in heaven. Give us this day our daily bread; and forgive us our trespasses as we forgive those who trespass against us; and lead us not into temptation, but deliver us from evil. Amen.

The Our Father (new ecumenical version)

Our Father in heaven, holy be your name, your kingdom come, your will be done on earth as in heaven. Give us today our daily bread. Forgive us our sins as we forgive those who sin against us. Do not bring us to the test but deliver us from evil. For the kingdom, the power, and the glory are yours now and forever.

The Hail Mary

Hail Mary, full of grace, the Lord is with you! Blessed are you among women, and blessed is the fruit of your womb, Jesus. Holy Mary, mother of God, pray for us sinners, now and at the hour of our death. Amen.

The Doxology

Glory be to the Father, and to the Son, and to the Holy Spirit, as it was in the beginning, is now, and ever shall be, world without end. Amen.

The Apostles' Creed

I believe in God the Father Almighty, creator of heaven and earth; and in Jesus Christ, his only Son, our Lord; who was conceived by the Holy Spirit, born of the Virgin Mary, suffered under Pontius Pilate, was crucified, died, and was buried. He descended into hell; the third day he arose again from the dead; he ascended into heaven and sits at the right hand of God the Father Almighty; from thence he shall come to judge the living and the dead. I believe in the Holy Spirit, the holy catholic church, the communion of saints, the forgiveness of sins, the resurrection of the body, and life everlasting. Amen.

An Act of Contrition

My God, I am sorry for my sins with all my heart. In choosing to do wrong and failing to do good, I have sinned against you whom I should love above all things. I firmly intend, with your help, to do penance, to sin no more, and to avoid whatever leads me to sin. Our Savior Jesus Christ suffered and died for us. In his name, my God, have mercy.

Grace before Meals

Bless us, O Lord, and these your gifts, which we are about to receive from your bounty, through Christ our Lord. Amen.

Grace after Meals

We give you thanks, O Lord, for all your gifts which we have received from your bounty, through Christ our Lord. Amen.

THE TEN COMMANDMENTS

The full text is found in the Bible in two places: in Exodus 20:1-7 and in Deuteronomy 5:6-21. Christians generally learn an abridged version of these, with slight differences between Catholics and Protestants. This is the arrangement used by Catholics.

1. I am the Lord your God; you shall have no other gods before me.

2. You shall not take the name of the Lord your God in vain.

3. Remember the sabbath day, to keep it holy.

4. Honor your father and your mother.

5. You shall not kill.

6. You shall not commit adultery.

7. You shall not steal.

8. You shall not bear false witness against your neighbor.

9. You shall not covet your neighbor's wife.

10. You shall not covet your neighbor's goods.